# Love From Above

By Jaime Lori Troiano

Illustrated by Judie Cavanaugh

Butterfly Wings Publishing Co.

Butterfly Wings Publishing Company
Norwalk, CT 06851
ButterflyWingsPublishing.com

ISBN: 978-0-692-04328-8

Library of Congress Catalog Number: 2018912774

Printed in the United States

# Dedication

To my mother, Lori,
you are the epitome of a strong woman who taught me
the meaning of unconditional love and unwavering support.
You instilled in me the belief that I can accomplish anything.
I will never understand how you did it, Mom.
Thank you, for everything.

# Instructions for Readers

Dear Reader,

This book was written with the intention of allowing you to personalize it so your deceased loved one can impart heartfelt messages of comfort to the intended reader(s).

You will see a space to write the name of the intended reader(s) at the beginning of the book and a space to write the name (or relationship) of the deceased near the end of the book. In addition, there is a space for you to paste pictures of your deceased loved one so he or she may always remain a part of this book.

It is my hope that this book brings comfort, peace, and a sense of closeness to all of you, as it did for my children and me.

Jaime Lori Troiano
2018

_____)
it was an honor to be

the first one to hold you,

even before you were born.

I was the first

to kiss your sweet cheeks,

tickle your chubby toes,

and look into your bright eyes.

The first time I gazed into your eyes,
I shared a piece of my soul with you.
You make me proud every day,
and your laughter brings
a gentle warmth to my heart.

When my spirit touched yours,
I felt your power,
        your determination,
        your generosity,
        and your abundance of love.

While you sleep at night,
we will dance together in your dreams.

Always show strength
and the courage to stand up
for what you believe in.
When you feel that you stand alone,
I will be there next to you.

Remember that you are perfectly you,
and to stay true to yourself,
not what others may want you to be.

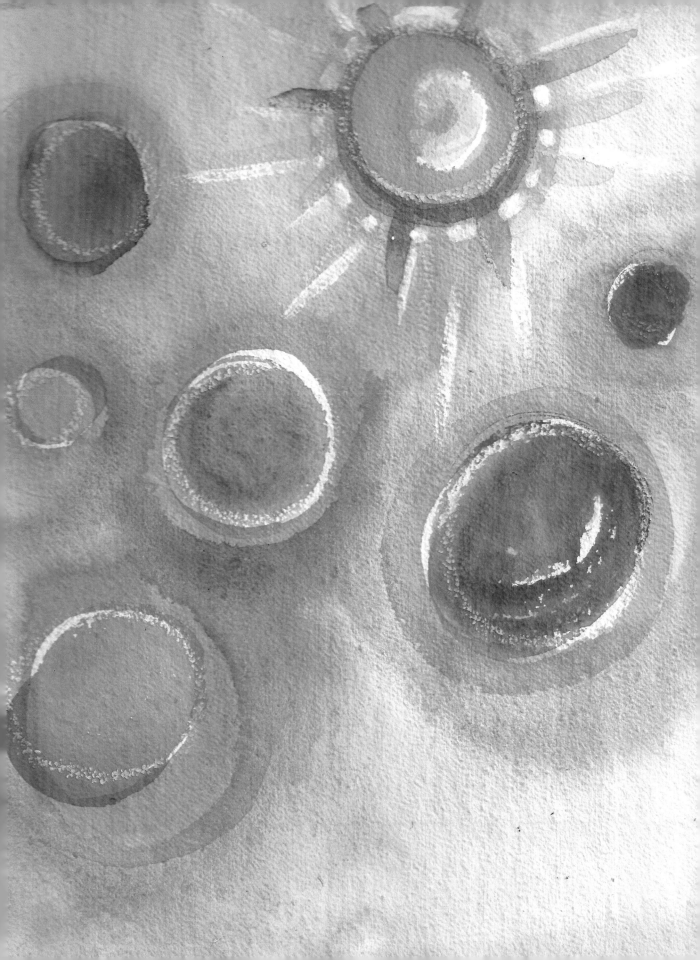

I am honored to be your guardian angel.
I promise to do my best
to guide you, protect you,
and shine the sun on you every day.

I wish for you to dream big,

            love deeply,

            and choose kindness.

            Always.

Thank you for choosing me to be

your _____

and know that I love you

forever and forever,

with my whole heart!

Paste photos of your loved one
in the frames provided.

## ACKNOWLEDGMENTS

Thank you to everyone who helped to make
my dream become a reality.

To Lorraine, who believed in this book when others didn't.
Without your invaluable expertise and guidance, this book
would never have come to life.

To Lorie, your creative mind and ability to take all the pieces
and put them together is amazing. I greatly appreciate your
talents and exceptional graphic design expertise.

To Judie, the one who shared my vision and hope
for this book. Your ability to transform words into
magnificent artwork amazes me, and I am so grateful
for your friendship and partnership.

***To my three favorites:***

Tricia, my better half, you always stop to listen to me,
no matter how many times I interrupt what you're doing.
Thanks for putting up with me and keeping me grounded;
your patience is not something that can be underestimated.

My two children, you will always be my little babies,
no matter how big you get. You gave me the inspiration
to create this book. Your Grandma Lori is your guardian angel
and is radiating her love from above.

You three are my reason for everything
and I love you all with my whole heart, forever and forever.

# Jaime Troiano

Having lost her mother at the age of twenty-three, Jaime struggled with the absence of the strongest figure in her life. Once Jaime became a mother of two beautiful children, she fully understood the powerful love a parent has for their children. Becoming a motherless mother proved to be difficult for Jaime and she wanted to impart some of her mother's wisdom onto her children. Thus, *Love from Above* was born.

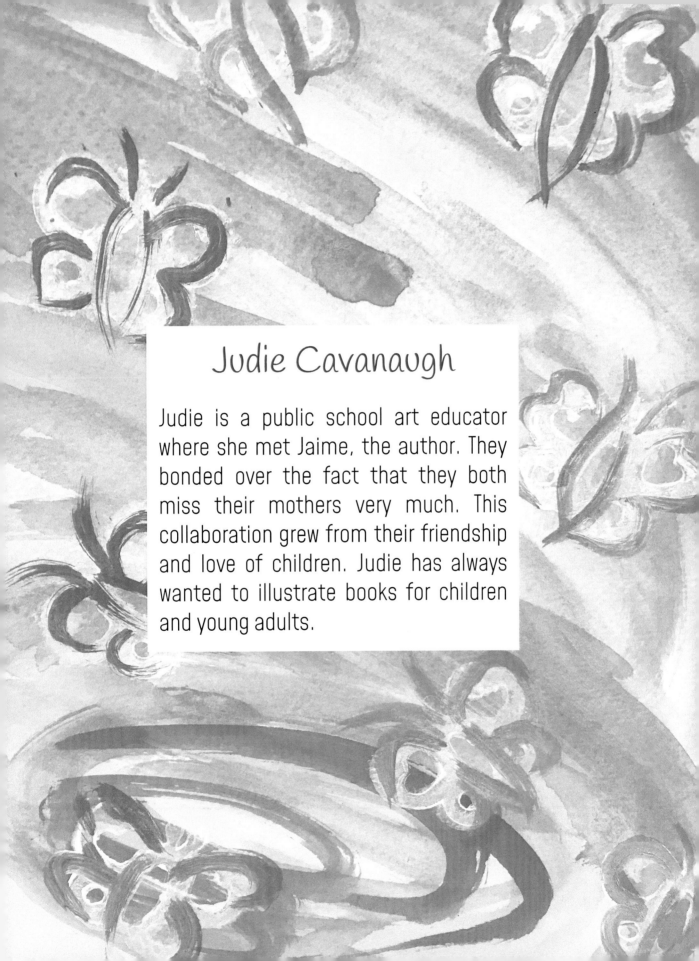

# Judie Cavanaugh

Judie is a public school art educator where she met Jaime, the author. They bonded over the fact that they both miss their mothers very much. This collaboration grew from their friendship and love of children. Judie has always wanted to illustrate books for children and young adults.